BRAIN GAMES

BIBLE

TRIVIA PUZZLES

Publications International, Ltd.

Brain Games is a registered trademark of Publications International, Ltd.
Copyright © 2018 Publications International, Ltd. All rights reserved. This
book may not be reproduced or quoted in whole or in part by any means
whatsoever without written permission from:

Louis Weber, CEO
Publications International, Ltd.
8140 Lehigh Avenue
Morton Grove, Illinois 60053

Permission is never granted for commercial purposes.

ISBN: 978-1-64030-313-3

Manufactured in U.S.A.

8 7 6 5 4 3 2 1

TABLE OF CONTENTS

TEST YOUR BIBLE TRIVIA KNOWLEDGE!

Generation after generation, the Bible continues to inspire, puzzle, instruct, and fascinate readers. But how well do you really know this famous text?

Divided into 12 chapters, *Bible Trivia Puzzles* offers more than 250 multiple-choice and true-false questions about Bible characters, places, and events. Chapters include Remedies and Miracles, Songs and Celebrations, Names and Numbers, Travels by Land and Water, and Son of God.

Some questions are easy, while others will likely stump readers. Answers to all questions are found on the following pages, along with references and additional information.

Are you ready? Turn the page and begin testing your Bible trivia knowledge, and don't forget to have fun!

NAMES AND NUMBERS

1. Which Old Testament character had 1,400 chariots and 12,000 horsemen?

A. Saul
B. Noah
C. Moses
D. Solomon

2. Who was NOT an Old Testament prophet?

A. Isaiah
B. Daniel
C. Silas
D. Jeremiah

Answers on page 6.

Answers from previous page:

1. D. Solomon. See 1 Kings 10:26.

2. C. Silas. The prophet Silas appears in the New Testament only. See Acts 15:32.

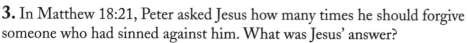

3. In Matthew 18:21, Peter asked Jesus how many times he should forgive someone who had sinned against him. What was Jesus' answer?

    A. 120
    B. 340
    C. 490
    D. 9,260

4. This prophetess was the wife of Lapidoth.

    A. Esther
    B. Anna
    C. Elisabeth
    D. Deborah

5. By what name was the disciple Tabitha also known?

    A. Dorcas
    B. Tamar
    C. Susanna
    D. Anna

Answers on page 8.

Answers from previous page:

3. C. 490. See Matthew 18:21–22.

4. D. Deborah. See Judges 4:4.

5. A. Dorcas. The disciple Tabitha, who is also called Dorcas, is described as a woman "full of good works and almsdeeds." See Acts 9:36.

6. What name did Pharaoh give to Joseph?

   A. Pithom

   B. Potipherah

   C. Misrephothmaim

   D. Zaphnathpaaneah

7. What new name did God give to Jacob?

   A. Israel

   B. Abraham

   C. Saul

   D. Mohammed

8. What married couple did Paul become friends with at Corinth?

   A. Lamech and Adah

   B. Joseph and Asenath

   C. Aquila and Priscilla

   D. Felix and Drusilla

Answers on page 10.

Answers from previous page:

6. D. Zaphnathpaaneah. See Genesis 41:45.

7. A. Israel. See Genesis 35:10.

8. C. Aquila and Priscilla. See Acts 18:1–2.

9. How many concubines did King Solomon have?

    A. 55

    B. 100

    C. 300

    D. 700

10. Job's children were killed in Job 1:13–20. How many sons and daughters did Job have?

    A. Seven sons and three daughters

    B. Nine sons and two daughters

    C. Ten sons and no daughters

    D. The number is unknown.

11. What young man rebuked Job's friends?

    A. Isaac

    B. Elihu

    C. Caleb

    D. Uriah

Answers on page 12.

Answers from previous page:

9. C. 300. In addition to 300 concubines, King Solomon had 700 wives. See 1 Kings 11:3.

10. A. Seven sons and three daughters. See Job 1:1–2.

11. B. Elihu. See Job 32.

12. What name appears in the shortest Bible verse?

    A. Eve
    B. Jesus
    C. Moses
    D. Job

13. Which angel announced the birth of John the Baptist?

    A. Michael
    B. Raphael
    C. Gabriel
    D. The angel isn't named.

14. Samuel was brought as a child to Shiloh to serve with this person.

    A. Eli
    B. Simon
    C. Paul
    D. John

Answers on page 14.

Answers from previous page:

12. B. Jesus. The shortest Bible verse is just two words: "Jesus wept." See John 11:35.

13. C. Gabriel. The angel Gabriel appeared to Zacharias and told him that his wife, Elisabeth, would bear a son to be named John. See Luke 1:13, 19.

14. A. Eli. After Samuel was born and weaned, his mother Hannah brought him to Shiloh to serve with Eli. See 1 Samuel 1:24–25.

15. Which king of Israel ruled for only seven days?

    A. Zimri
    B. David
    C. Ahab
    D. Cyrus

16. What was the name of the family member who raised Esther?

    A. Naboth
    B. Dorcas
    C. Haggar
    D. Mordecai

17. Who was the Bible's oldest man?

    A. Methuselah
    B. Enosh
    C. Lamech
    D. Abraham

Answers on page 16.

Answers from previous page:

15. A. Zimri. See 1 Kings 16:15. Zimri burned down the palace in 1 Kings 16:18 and died in the fire.

16. D. Mordecai. When Esther's parents died, an older cousin named Mordecai took her in and raised her as his own daughter. See Esther 2:7.

17. A. Methuselah. Methuselah lived to be 969 years old. See Genesis 5:27.

18. The second-oldest man in the Bible lived to be 962.

    A. True
    B. False

19. Which king went insane and ate grass?

    A. Jehu
    B. Hezekiah
    C. Nebuchadnezzar
    D. Zechariah

20. What is the longest name in the Bible?

    A. Bashanhavothjairi
    B. Kibrothhattaavahneah
    C. Mahershalalhashbaz
    D. Abelbethmaachah

Answers on page 18.

Answers from previous page:

18. A. True. Jared, the second-oldest man in the Bible, lived to the age of 962. See Genesis 5:20.

19. C. Nebuchadnezzar. He was driven from men and ate grass "like oxen." See Daniel 4:33.

20. C. Mahershalalhashbaz. See Isaiah 8:1.

21. Who was the king of Bashan?

    A. Hoshea

    B. Og

    C. Josiah

    D. Tibni

22. Which woman was Zidonian?

    A. Jezebel

    B. Deborah

    C. Hagar

    D. Delilah

23. How many people did Jesus raise from the dead?

    A. One

    B. Three

    C. Four

    D. Eight

Answers on page 20.

Answers from previous page:

21. B. Og. See Numbers 21:33.

22. A. Jezebel. See 1 Kings 16:31.

23. B. Three. Jesus raised three people from the dead. He raised the son of a widow from Nain when he encountered his funeral procession. Then he raised the 12-year-old daughter of Jairus. And finally he raised his friend Lazarus, the brother of Mary and Martha. See Luke 7:11–15, 8:41–56; Matthew 9:18–25; Mark 5:21–42; and John 11:1–44.

24. In the Parable of the Lost Sheep, how many sheep did the shepherd have?

    A. 12

    B. 40

    C. 100

    D. A flock—the number isn't specified.

25. In the Parable of the Rich Man and Lazarus, the Rich Man talked to this person after death.

    A. Lazarus

    B. An angel of the Lord

    C. Moses

    D. Abraham

26. In the Parable of the Ten Virgins, how many were foolish and how many were wise?

    A. Nine were foolish and one was wise.

    B. Seven were foolish and three were wise.

    C. Five were foolish and five were wise.

    D. All were foolish.

Answers on page 22.

Answers from previous page:

24. C. 100. See Matthew 18:12–13 and Luke 15:4–6.

25. D. Abraham. See Luke 16:19-31.

26. C. Five were foolish and five were wise. See Matthew 25:1–13.

27. How many children did Adam have?

A. Two
B. Three
C. Four
D. An unknown number

28. When the Lord appeared to Abram to make the covenant of circumcision and change his name to Abraham, how old was Abram?

A. 90 years old
B. 99 years old
C. 100 years old
D. The Bible doesn't say.

29. Genesis 5, which lists the descendants of Adam through Noah, says, "And Enoch walked with God: and he was not; for God took him." How old was Enoch when this happened?

A. 365 years
B. 930 years
C. 969 years
D. The Bible doesn't say.

Answers on page 24.

Answers from previous page:

27. D. An unknown number. Cain, Abel, and Seth are the only named children, but Genesis 5:4 says, "And the days of Adam after he had begotten Seth were eight hundred years: and he begat sons and daughters."

28. B. 99 years old. See Genesis 17:1.

29. A. 365 years. See Genesis 5:21–24.

30. Who was Timothy's grandmother?

    A. Eunice

    B. Merab

    C. Lois

    D. Elisabeth

31. Who is called Reuel in Exodus 2:18 and Hobab in Numbers 10:29?

    A. Ishmael

    B. Hezekiel

    C. Reuben

    D. Jethro

32. Who was taken up to heaven in a chariot of fire?

    A. Elijah

    B. Daniel

    C. Sisera

    D. Nathan

Answers on page 26.

Answers from previous page:

30. C. Lois. Timothy was inspired and influenced by the "unfeigned faith" of his grandmother, Lois, and his mother, Eunice. See 2 Timothy 1:5.

31. D. Jethro. Moses' father-in-law, Jethro, had other names. In Exodus, he is initially referred to as Reuel (2:16–18), priest of Midian and father of seven daughters, but then as Jethro (3:1). In Numbers 10:29, the same man is called "Hobab, the son of Raguel the Midianite." See Exodus 2:16–21, 3:1, 4:18; Numbers 10:29; and Judges 4:11.

32. A. Elijah. See 2 Kings 2:11.

33. How many prophets of Baal did Jezebel support?

    A. 62
    B. 170
    C. 450
    D. 1,000

34. How many men did Moses send to explore Canaan?

    A. Two
    B. 12
    C. 36
    D. 100

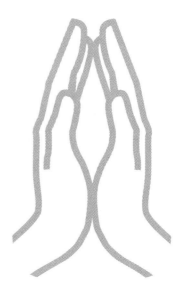

35. How many "minor prophets" are there?

    A. Five
    B. Seven
    C. 12
    D. 14

Answers on page 28.

Answers from previous page:

33. C. 450. See 1 Kings 18:19.

34. B. 12. Moses was commanded to send out one man from each of the 12 tribes of Israel to explore the land of Canaan. See Numbers 13:1—16.

35. C. 12. The "minor prophets" make up the final 12 books of the Old Testament. See Hosea 1:1—Malachi 4:6.

MOTHERS AND FATHERS, SONS AND DAUGHTERS

1. Who was Hannah's firstborn child?

A. Miriam
B. Joseph
C. John
D. Samuel

2. Who was the third son of Adam and Eve?

A. Micah
B. Shem
C. Abel
D. Seth

Answers on page 30.

Answers from previous page:

1. D. Samuel. See 1 Samuel 1:20.

2. D. Seth. Eve said God "appointed me another seed instead of Abel, whom Cain slew." See Genesis 4:25.

3. Which woman gave birth to Moses?

    A. Miriam
    B. Jochebed
    C. Zipporah
    D. Dinah

4. This king forced his son to pass through fire.

    A. Solomon
    B. Manasseh
    C. Jehoshaphat
    D. Hezekiah

5. Which was NOT a daughter-father pair?

    A. Leah and Laban
    B. Merab and Saul
    C. Gomer and Hosea
    D. Jezebel and Ethbaal

Answers on page 32.

Answers from previous page:

3. B. Jochebed. After hiding him for three months, Jochebed put Moses in an "ark of bulrushes" by the river. When the pharaoh's daughter found the basket, Miriam, Moses' sister, stepped forward and offered to find a Hebrew nurse for the child. Jochebed was paid to nurse her own son until he was weaned. See Exodus 2:2–10.

4. B. Manasseh. Forcing his son to pass through fire was just one of Manasseh's many wicked deeds that angered the Lord. Manasseh also "used enchantments, and dealt with familiar spirits and wizards." See 2 Kings 21:1–6.

5. C. Gomer and Hosea. Gomer was Hosea's wife, not daughter. See Hosea 1:2–4. For other daughter-father pairs, see Genesis 29:16, 1 Samuel 18:17, and 1 Kings 16:31.

6. Who were the two sons of Naomi and Elimelech?

    A. James and John
    B. Mahlon and Chilion
    C. Esau and Obed
    D. Ham and Shem

7. Which Old Testament character was willing to sacrifice his son on an altar to God?

    A. Moses
    B. Adam
    C. Isaac
    D. Abraham

8. Who was the mother of Zimran, Jokshan, Medan, Midian, Ishbak, and Shuah?

    A. Naomi
    B. Adah
    C. Keturah
    D. Tamar

Answers on page 34.

Answers from previous page:

6. B. Mahlon and Chilion. The sons married two women of Moab, Ruth, and Orpah. See Ruth 1:2–4.

7. D. Abraham. See James 2:21–22.

8. C. Keturah. After Sarah's death, Abraham took Keturah as a wife. She gave birth to six sons, including Midian, ancestor of the Midianites. See Genesis 25:1–2.

MOTHERS AND FATHERS, SONS AND DAUGHTERS

9. Which disciple was asked to look after Mary, mother of Jesus, after Jesus' death?

A. James (son of Zebedee)
B. John
C. (Simon) Peter
D. James (son of Alphaeus)

10. What did the mother of James and John ask of Jesus?

A. To heal her "blood problem"
B. To sit her sons on Jesus' right and left hands in the kingdom
C. To cast out her demons
D. To allow her to wash his feet

11. Which angel appeared to Mary to tell her she was chosen to give birth to the Son of God?

A. Raphael
B. Gabriel
C. Lucifer
D. The angel isn't named.

Answers on page 36.

Answers from previous page:

9. B. John. As a sort of last will and testament, Jesus asked from the cross that his disciple John look after his mother, saying, "behold thy son" to Mary and "behold thy mother" to John. John took Mary into his own home. See John 19:26–27.

10. B. To sit her sons on Jesus' right and left hands in the kingdom. See Matthew 20:20–21.

11. B. Gabriel. See Luke 1:26–32.

MOTHERS AND FATHERS, SONS AND DAUGHTERS

12. Which of the following was a mother-son pair?

    A. Rebekah and Moses
    B. Leah and Esau
    C. Jochebed and Seth
    D. Bathsheba and Solomon

13. Lot was the father of two of his grandchildren.

    A. True
    B. False

14. Which child was born to a maid of Abraham's wife?

    A. Esau
    B. John
    C. Ishmael
    D. Isaac

Answers on page 38.

Answers from previous page:

12. D. Bathsheba and Solomon. See 2 Samuel 24:24. Later, in 1 Chronicles 3:5, Solomon's mother is called Bathshua.

13. A. True. Lot was the father of two of his grandchildren—Moab and Benammi. To preserve the seed of their father, both of Lot's daughters each had a son by him. See Genesis 19:36–38.

14. C. Ishmael. Because Abraham's wife, Sarah, could not bear a child, she offered her maid, Hagar, as a surrogate. Hagar gave birth to Ishmael. See Genesis 16:15.

MOTHERS AND FATHERS, SONS AND DAUGHTERS

15. Which of the following was a father-son pair?

    A. Mahlon and Amnon
    B. Isaac and Ishmael
    C. Joseph and Manasseh
    D. Abraham and Reuben

16. Who was the father of Tamar's twin sons?

    A. Er
    B. Judah
    C. Onan
    D. Shelah

17. Whose mother was told to drink no wine during her pregnancy?

    A. Samson
    B. Jesus
    C. Caleb
    D. John the Baptist

Answers on page 40.

Answers from previous page:

15. C. Joseph and Manasseh. See Genesis 41:51.

16. B. Judah. Tamar disguised herself, pretended to be a harlot, and lured her father-in-law, Judah. Tamar demanded Judah's signet as a pledge of payment. A pregnant Tamar was brought before Judah for punishment. When Judah saw his signet and realized he was the father, he repented. See Genesis 38:6–26.

17. A. Samson. Samson's mother was instructed not to drink wine or eat unclean things during her pregnancy. And once her son was born, no razor was ever to be used on Samson's head. See Judges 13:2–24.

18. Jacob favored his eldest son, Reuben.

    A. True

    B. False

19. Which woman did NOT have children with Jacob?

    A. Rebekah

    B. Leah

    C. Zilpah

    D. Rachel

20. Which set of twins wrestled in the womb of their mother?

    A. Samson and Joash

    B. Jacob and Esau

    C. Manasseh and Micah

    D. Isaac and Ishmael

Answers on page 42.

Answers from previous page:

18. B. False. Jacob favored Joseph more than Reuben and all his children, as he was the "son of his old age." See Genesis 37:1–3.

19. A. Rebekah. See Genesis 35:23–26.

20. B. Jacob and Esau. When the once-barren Rebekah finally conceived, the children "struggled together within her." The Lord told Rebekah that there were two nations in her womb, and the one people would be stronger than the other, and the elder would serve the younger. See Genesis 25:21–26.

21. Shechem, the son of Hamor the Hivite, who fell in love with Jacob's daughter, Dinah, married her after he had "defiled" her to erase her shame.

  A. True
  B. False

22. Timothy was the son of a Jewish mother and a Greek father.

  A. True
  B. False

23. Ruth accompanied her mother-in-law Naomi from Moab to this town.

  A. Nazareth
  B. Bethlehem
  C. Joppa
  D. Beersheba

Answers on page 44.

Answers from previous page:

21. B. False. After raping Dinah, Shechem told his father to "Get me this damsel to wife." Hamor suggested to Jacob that their tribes intermarry. Jacob's sons, furious that their sister had been defiled, demanded all males in Hamor's tribe be circumcised before they could marry Israelite women. Three days after the circumcisions, Dinah's brothers killed Shechem, Hamor, and all the men of their city. See Genesis 34:1–26.

22. A. True. See Acts 16:1.

23. B. Bethlehem. See Ruth 1:19.

MOTHERS AND FATHERS, SONS AND DAUGHTERS

24. What were the occupations of the sons of Zebedee before they met Jesus?

    A. Tax collector and silversmith
    B. Shepherds
    C. Priest and merchant
    D. Fishers

25. The sons of Bilhah were Gad and Asher.

    A. True
    B. False

26. David's best friend was the son of King Saul.

    A. True
    B. False

Answers on page 46.

Answers from previous page:

24. D. Fishers. James and John, the sons of Zebedee, were fishermen. James and John were in a ship with their father mending their nets when called by Jesus. See Matthew 4:21.

25. B. False. The sons of Bilhah, Rachel's handmaid, were Dan and Naphtali. Gad and Asher were the sons of Zilpah, Leah's handmaid. See Genesis 35:25–26.

26. A. True. David's best friend was Jonathan, the son of King Saul. 1 Samuel 18:1 says, "the soul of Jonathan was knit with the soul of David, and Jonathan loved him as his own soul."

27. Who was the offspring of Tamar?

    A. Pharez
    B. Ezekiel
    C. Laban
    D. Athaliah

28. Solomon was the son of King David and Queen Jezebel.

    A. True
    B. False

29. King Jehoiakim was the son of King Josiah.

    A. True
    B. False

Answers on page 48.

Answers from previous page:

27. A. Pharez. Tamar had twin sons, the elder of which, Pharez, was an ancestor of Jesus. See Genesis 38:24–30.

28. B. False. Solomon was the son of David and Bathsheba. See 2 Samuel 12:24.

29. A. True. See Jeremiah 1:3.

SETTLEMENTS, NEAR AND FAR

1. What was the name of the first town Lot came to after fleeing Sodom?

   A. Moab
   B. Zoar
   C. Tyre
   D. Zobah

2. The Apostle Paul was born in this city.

   A. Tarah
   B. Tamar
   C. Thyatira
   D. Tarsus

Answers on page 50.

Answers from previous page:

1. B. Zoar. See Genesis 19:19–23.

2. D. Tarsus. Tarsus was a city of Cilicia, an area now part of modern-day Turkey. See Acts 21:39.

3. This city was also known as the city of palm trees.

   A. Jericho
   B. Jerusalem
   C. Damascus
   D. Gilgal

4. Shishak, king of Egypt, was notable for taking away this city's treasure, including Solomon's golden shields.

   A. Joppa
   B. Dan
   C. Capernaum
   D. Jerusalem

5. Nebuchadnezzar was king of this city.

   A. Sparta
   B. Athens
   C. Babylon
   D. Assyria

Answers on page 52.

Answers from previous page:

3. A. Jericho. It is described as the city of palm trees in Deuteronomy 34:3 and Judges 1:16, 3:13.

4. D. Jerusalem. See 2 Chronicles 12:9.

5. C. Babylon. This king of Babylon is mentioned in multiple places in the Bible. His sack of Jerusalem, for example, is related in 2 Kings 24.

6. 1 Corinthians was written by Paul to fellow Christians in Corinth. Where was the city of Corinth located?

    A. France

    B. On the Nile River

    C. On a small island near Rhodes

    D. Greece

7. Which city did John watch descend from heaven?

    A. New Rome

    B. Babylon

    C. New Jerusalem

    D. Ur

8. The Israelites were forced to build cities while in bondage in Egypt. What is the name of one of those cities?

    A. Cairo

    B. Raamses

    C. Alexandria

    D. Calah

Answers on page 54.

Answers from previous page:

6. D. Greece. The ancient city of Corinth was located on the narrow isthmus that connects the Peloponnese peninsula to the mainland.

7. C. New Jerusalem. In Revelation 21:2, John describes the holy city "coming down from God out of heaven, prepared as a bride adorned for her husband."

8. B. Raamses. See Exodus 1:11.

9. Which city was Abram originally from?

   A. Oreb

   B. Ur

   C. Uz

   D. Haran

10. The Apostle Philip was originally from the town of Gaza.

   A. True

   B. False

11. What is the name of the city founded by Cain?

   A. Nineveh

   B. Nod

   C. Enoch

   D. Gog

Answers on page 56.

Answers from previous page:

9. B. Ur. The ancient city of Ur was located near the mouth of the Euphrates on its western bank. See Genesis 11:31.

10. B. False. Philip's home is identified in John 1:44: "Now Philip was of Bethsaida, the city of Andrew and Peter."

11. C. Enoch. Cain named the city after his son. See Genesis 4:17.

12. Moab is frequently in conflict with Israel in the Old Testament. Where was this kingdom located?

    A. East of the Dead Sea

    B. It overlapped with Lebanon.

    C. Somewhere in the Arabian Desert

    D. Turkey

13. While sailing to Italy, Paul's ship was driven off course and shipwrecked on this island.

    A. Melita

    B. Crete

    C. Clauda

    D. Patmos

14. When the Jews decided to kill Saul in Acts 9, he escaped this city by being lowered from its walls in a basket.

    A. Jerusalem

    B. Damascus

    C. Rome

    D. Bethlehem

Answers on page 58.

Answers from previous page:

12. A. East of the Dead Sea.

13. A. Melita. The island is now known as Malta. See Acts 28:1.

14. B. Damascus. See Acts 9:25.

15. The book of Daniel tells the story of Nebuchadnezzar's siege of this city.

    A. Jerusalem
    B. Babylon
    C. Gomorrah
    D. Ai

16. God told Moses that his people would take possession of this land and drive out its inhabitants.

    A. Assyria
    B. Syria
    C. Canaan
    D. Lebanon

17. The Israelites conquered Jerusalem under King David. What was the name of the city at that time?

    A. Salem
    B. Jebus
    C. Syon
    D. Bethel

Answers on page 60.

Answers from previous page:

15. A. Jerusalem. See Daniel 1:1.

16. C. Canaan. See Numbers 33:50–53.

17. B. Jebus. See 1 Chronicles 11:4.

18. Jesus was crucified at Golgotha, outside this city.

    A. Heliopolis
    B. Nazareth
    C. Jerusalem
    D. Rome

19. God divided the single language of humanity into many languages in this city.

    A. Ur-Baal
    B. Babel
    C. Shem
    D. Zoar

20. Jacob was traveling from Beersheba toward Haran when he stopped for the night and dreamed of the ladder of heaven. What did he name the place where he stayed?

    A. Bethlehem
    B. Bethel
    C. Bethany
    D. Bethharan

Answers on page 62.

Answers from previous page:

18. C. Jerusalem. See John 19:20.

19. B. Babel. See Genesis 11:7–9.

20. B. Bethel. Genesis 28:19 explains, "And he called the name of that place Bethel: but the name of that city was called Luz at the first."

21. This was the first city in which Jesus' followers were referred to as Christians.

A. Rome

B. Syracuse

C. Antioch

D. Athensny

22. Joseph told Pharaoh in Genesis 47:1 that his family had come to the land of Goshen. What modern country would Goshen be within?

A. Turkey

B. Greece

C. Egypt

D. Saudi Arabia

23. Acts and Galatians both mention a place named Cilicia. What was Cilicia?

A. A small town

B. A capital city of Greece

C. A coastal region

D. The continent of Europe

Answers on page 64.

Answers from previous page:

21. C. Antioch. See Acts 11:26.

22. C. Egypt.

23. C. A coastal region. It was located in southern Turkey, along the coast of the Mediterranean Sea.

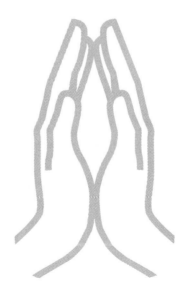

24. In Luke 4:24, Jesus tells the synagogue, "No prophet is accepted in his own country." The people he addressed lived in this city.

    A. Capernaum

    B. Nazareth

    C. Jerusalem

    D. Samaria

25. Jesus visited and stayed at Capernaum several times. What was this town's location?

    A. On the shore of the Dead Sea

    B. On the shore of the Sea of Galilee

    C. On the Mediterranean coast

    D. On the banks of the Jordan River

26. India is mentioned twice in the Bible.

    A. True

    B. False

Answers on page 66.

Answers from previous page:

24. B. Nazareth. See Luke 4:16.

25. B. On the shore of the Sea of Galilee. Capernaum was on its northern coast.

26. A. True. Esther 1:1 mentions a ruler named Ahasuerus who ruled "from India even unto Ethiopia." Esther 8:9 also mentions provinces of India.

MOUNTAINS, RIVERS, VALLEYS, AND SEAS

1. Joshua brought the Israelites into the Promised Land across this body of water.

   A. The Persian Gulf
   B. The Jordan River
   C. The Dead Sea
   D. The Nile River

2. The prophet Ezra proclaimed a fast at this river.

   A. The Nile River
   B. The Jordan River
   C. The Ahava River
   D. The Euphrates River

Answers on page 68.

Answers from previous page:

1. B. The Jordan River. Strictly speaking, they crossed the Jordan's riverbed. Joshua 3:17 notes that the "Israelites passed over on dry ground."

2. C. The Ahava River. See Ezra 8:21.

3. What body of water did God part so that Israel could escape the Egyptians?

    A. The Red Sea
    B. The Dead Sea
    C. The Nile River
    D. None of the above

4. Moses received the stone tablets containing the Ten Commandments on this mountain.

    A. Mount Zion
    B. Mount Sinai
    C. Mount Serbal
    D. The mountain is unknown.

5. Where was Joshua buried?

    A. On a hill
    B. Between two mountains
    C. In a valley
    D. At the foot of Mount Zion

Answers on page 70.

Answers from previous page:

3. A. The Red Sea. See Exodus 14:21.

4. B. Mount Sinai. See Exodus 31:18.

5. A. On a hill. Judges 2:9 says, "And they buried him in the border of his inheritance in Timnathheres, in the mount of Ephraim, on the north side of the hill Gaash."

6. Mount Hermon is frequently referred to in the Old Testament. Where is it located?

   A. To the south, on Egypt's border
   B. To the north, on Lebanon's border

7. Moses commanded his people to pronounce 12 curses on this mountain.

   A. Mount Ebal
   B. Mount Gerizim
   C. Mount Hermon
   D. Mount Carmel

8. From which mountain was Moses allowed to see the Promised Land?

   A. Mount Horeb
   B. Mount Ararat
   C. Mount Nebo
   D. Mount Bashan

Answers on page 72.

Answers from previous page:

6. B. To the north, on Lebanon's border. This snowy mountain's highest peak is about 9,232 feet (2,814 meters).

7. A. Mount Ebal. See Deuteronomy 27:11–26.

8. C. Mount Nebo. See Deuteronomy 32:49.

9. The mountainous region of Moriah was the setting for this biblical event.

   A. Where Moses saw the Promised Land
   B. Where Abraham died
   C. Where God revealed himself to Moses
   D. Where Abraham was called to sacrifice his son

10. Elijah challenged the priests of Baal to demonstrate that their god would light a fire on their altar. After they failed, he called on God to ignite his own offering and succeeded. Where did this take place?

   A. Mount Carmel
   B. Aphek
   C. Mount Zion
   D. On a hill near Jericho

11. What is the name of the mountain that Moses was near when the angel of the Lord appeared to him in a burning bush?

   A. Carmel
   B. Nebo
   C. Tabor
   D. Horeb

Answers on page 74.

Answers from previous page:

9. D. Where Abraham was called to sacrifice his son. God relents in Genesis 22:12: "And he said, Lay not thine hand upon the lad, neither do thou any thing unto him: for now I know that thou fearest God, seeing thou hast not withheld thy son, thine only son from me."

10. A. Mount Carmel. See 1 Kings 18:19–38.

11. D. Horeb. See Exodus 3:1–2.

MOUNTAINS, RIVERS, VALLEYS, AND SEAS

12. Elisha told a man to wash in this river seven times and his leprosy would be cured.

   A. The Abana River

   B. The Pharpar River

   C. The Jordan River

   D. The Damascus River

13. While in Athens, Paul called the men of the city superstitious. He did this on a hill named after this deity.

   A. Mars

   B. Athena

   C. The Unknown God

   D. Baal

14. God made the Moon stand still over this valley while Joshua and his soldiers defeated the Amorites.

   A. Megiddon

   B. Shittim

   C. Achor

   D. Ajalon

Answers on page 76.

Answers from previous page:

12. C. The Jordan River. See 2 Kings 5:10.

13. A. Mars. See Acts 17:22.

14. D. Ajalon. See Exodus 10:12.

15. Where did Noah's ark come to rest after the Flood?

    A. Mount Everest
    B. The mountains of Asir
    C. The mountains of Ararat
    D. The Bible does not give a location.

16. What is the name of the only mountain range in Israel that runs to the Mediterranean Sea?

    A. The Judean Hills
    B. Mount Carmel
    C. The Lebanon Mountains
    D. The Golan Heights

17. The Dead Sea, as its name implies, contains almost no life forms. Why?

    A. It is too acidic.
    B. Industrial runoff killed all the plants and fish.
    C. Its sulphur content is too high.
    D. Its salinity (saltiness) is too high.

Answers on page 78.

Answers from previous page:

15. C. The mountains of Ararat. See Genesis 8:4.

16. B. Mount Carmel. Though referred to as a single mountain, it is actually a series of mountainous ridges.

17. D. Its salinity (saltiness) is too high. The landlocked Dead Sea lies in a desert. When its waters evaporate in the heat, salty minerals are left behind, causing the remaining water to become saltier.

18. The four rivers associated with the garden of Eden are the Euphrates, Hiddekel, Gihon, and:

A. Nile River
B. Tigris River
C. Jordan River
D. Pison River

19. Israel is bordered to the west by this body of water.

A. The Mediterranean Sea
B. The Red Sea
C. The Jordan River
D. The Black Sea

20. The Sea of Galilee was also called:

A. Galilee was its only name.
B. The Great Salty Sea
C. The Middle Sea
D. The Sea of Tiberias

Answers on page 80.

Answers from previous page:

18. D. Pison River. See Genesis 2:11–14.

19. A. The Mediterranean Sea. In the Bible it is usually referred to as "the great sea." For example, Numbers 34:6 says, "And as for the western border, ye shall even have the great sea for a border: this shall be your west border."

20. D. The Sea of Tiberias. See John 6:1.

21. This river was the site of a battle between Israel (led by Barak) and the Canaanites (led by Sisera).

A. Merom
B. Siddim
C. Yarmuk
D. Kishon

22. David's army killed 18,000 Syrians in this valley.

A. Jezreel
B. The valley of salt
C. The valley of stones
D. Mizpeh

23. Mark 1:9 describes Jesus' baptism by John in the Jordan River. This small river runs south from the Sea of Galilee into what body of water?

A. The Red Sea
B. The Dead Sea
C. The Euphrates River
D. The Mediterranean Sea

Answers on page 82.

Answers from previous page:

21. D. Kishon. The prophet Deborah initiated this battle, telling Barak, "And I will draw unto thee to the river Kishon Sisera, the captain of Jabin's army, with his chariots and his multitude; and I will deliver him into thine hand," in Judges 4:7.

22. B. The valley of salt. See 2 Samuel 8:13. Several battles were fought in this location; king Amaziah's victory over the Edomites is mentioned in 2 Kings 14:7.

23. B. The Dead Sea. The Jordan River ends its run in this landlocked salt lake.

24. In Revelation, an angel pours out a vial on this river, causing it to dry up.

   A. The Jordan River
   B. The Euphrates River
   C. The Pishon River
   D. The Pharpar River

25. Lot and Abram separated after deciding the land could not support both of their herds. Where did Lot go?

   A. The plain of Jordan
   B. The valley of Achor
   C. The wilderness of Judaea
   D. A valley in Egypt

26. God once caused the streams, rivers, and ponds of this country to turn to blood.
   A. Jordan
   B. Canaan
   C. Babylon
   D. Egypt

Answers on page 84.

Answers from previous page:

24. B. The Euphrates River. See Revelation 16:12.

25. A. The plain of Jordan. Genesis 13:11 says, "Then Lot chose him all the plain of Jordan; and Lot journeyed east: and they separated themselves the one from the other."

26. D. Egypt. This was the first of the 10 plagues God inflicted on Egypt in the book of Exodus. See Exodus 7:19.

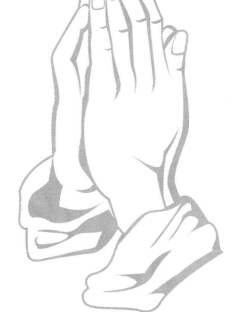

27. The word Jezreel sometimes refers to a:

A. Mountain
B. Valley

28. This valley is condemned several times in the Old Testament as a place of child sacrifice.

A. Gibeon
B. Beersheba
C. Hinnom
D. Jezreel

29. Mount Zion is mentioned in multiple places in the Bible. Where is it located?

A. Jericho
B. Jerusalem
C. On the edge of the Sinai Peninsula
D. Its location is unknown.

Answers on page 86.

Answers from previous page:

27. B. Valley. The Bible uses the word as a place name or valley, but never as a mountain. For example, see Joshua 17:16 and Judges 6:33.

28. C. Hinnom. Jeremiah 32:35 states, "And they built the high places of Baal, which are in the valley of the son of Hinnom, to cause their sons and their daughters to pass through the fire unto Molech." This valley was just outside ancient Jerusalem.

29. B. Jerusalem. It is also (more aptly) described as a hill, as in Psalm 2:6: "Yet have I set my king upon my holy hill of Zion." It has been the site of fortifications and settlements for centuries.

GIFTS, PAYMENTS, AND OTHER OFFERINGS

1. When Jacob's sons were preparing to return to Egypt, Jacob told them to bring gifts for Joseph, including these nuts. What were they?

A. Peanuts

B. Cashews

C. Almonds

D. Macadamia nuts

2. What meal did Boaz offer Ruth when they first met?

A. Bread dipped in vinegar

B. Bread dipped in olive oil

C. Honey

D. Corn

Answers on page 88.

Answers from previous page:

1. C. Almonds. See Genesis 43:11: "And their father Israel said unto them, If it must be so now, do this; take of the best fruits in the land in your vessels, and carry down the man a present, a little balm, and a little honey, spices, and myrrh, nuts, and almonds." Some translations list "pistachio nuts" ahead of almonds.

2. A. Bread dipped in vinegar. Ruth 2 tells of Boaz meeting Ruth, speaking to her of her kindness to Naomi, and offering her bread and vinegar at mealtime.

3. At Bethany, a woman anointed Jesus with costly perfume in a container of this material.

   A. Gold
   B. Silver
   C. Jade
   D. Alabaster

4. How much did King Omri pay for the hill of Samaria?

   A. He took it from King Asa.
   B. It was a gift from King Asa.
   C. Two bushels of gold
   D. Two talents of silver

5. In what city does Jesus cast the moneychangers out of the temple?

   A. Damascus
   B. Jericho
   C. Jerusalem
   D. Nazareth

Answers on page 90.

Answers from previous page:

3. D. Alabaster. See Matthew 26:7, Mark 14:3, and Luke 7:37. John's gospel account doesn't specify a material, although unlike the other gospels it does name the woman as Mary, sister of Martha and Lazarus. See John 12:2–8.

4. D. Two talents of silver. See 1 Kings 16:24.

5. C. Jerusalem. See Matthew 21:12, Mark 11:15, Luke 19:45, John 2:15.

6. Who promised to pay back the people he cheated four times over?

    A. Judas Iscariot
    B. Peter
    C. Simeon
    D. Zacchaeus

7. Who sought a bribe from Paul in Acts 24?

    A. Felix
    B. Jabin
    C. Cyrus
    D. Sheba

8. In the temple, Jesus praised the widow who put this little amount into the treasury.

    A. One coin
    B. Two coins
    C. Three coins
    D. A few coins—the Bible doesn't say the exact number

Answers on page 92.

Answers from previous page:

6. D. Zacchaeus. Zacchaeus promised before the Lord to give half of his goods to the poor and to restore any man he cheated fourfold. See Luke 19:8.

7. A. Felix. See Acts 24:24–26.

8. B. Two coins. See Mark 12:42 and Luke 21:2.

9. How many pieces of silver were given to Judas as a bribe to betray Jesus?

    A. 20

    B. 30

    C. 60

    D. 100

10. Which of the following was NOT a gift the queen of Sheba gave to Solomon in 1 Kings 10:10?

    A. Talents of gold

    B. Horses

    C. Spices

    D. Precious stones

11. What gift did the daughter of Herodias ask for after she danced for Herod?

    A. To conceive a child with her that would succeed him as king

    B. The head of John the Baptist

    C. The banishment of Baal worshippers

    D. The murder of her rival

Answers on page 94.

Answers from previous page:

9. B. 30. According to the Gospel of Matthew, Judas returned the 30 pieces of silver (before hanging himself), and the elders used it to buy a potter's field—a small plot filled with broken pottery and other trash that would be used to bury poor people. See Matthew 27:3–10.

10. B. Horses. Sheba brought King Solomon 120 talents of gold, a great store of spices, and precious stones, but no horses. See 1 Kings 10:10.

11. B. The head of John the Baptist. After dancing before Herod and pleasing him, Herodias's daughter asked for the head of John the Baptist. Herod kept his promise to give her whatever she asked for. John the Baptist was beheaded in the prison and his head was delivered to her in a charger. See Matthew 14:6–11 and Mark 6:21–28.

12. The gospels of Matthew and Mark tell of Jesus feeding a crowd of 4,000 with the following food.

    A. Five loaves and two fish, with 12 baskets left over

    B. Seven loaves and a few fish, with seven baskets left over

    C. Two loaves and five fish, with five baskets left over

    D. Seven loaves and seven fish, with nothing left over

13. In exile at the court of Nebuchadnezzar in Babylon, Daniel and his companions proposed to eat and drink these instead of partaking of the royal food and wine.

    A. Bread and grape juice

    B. Vegetables and water

    C. Honey and water

    D. Bread and wine

14. What did Abraham serve his three visitors who turned out to be sent by the Lord?

    A. Bread

    B. A calf

    C. Butter and milk

    D. All of the above

Answers on page 96.

Answers from previous page:

12. B. Seven loaves and a few fish, with seven baskets left over. See Matthew 15:32–39 and Mark 8:1–10. This is related as a separate event from the feeding of the 5,000 with five loaves and two fish. For that event, see Matthew 14:13–21, Mark 6:31–44, Luke 9:10–17, and John 6:5–15.

13. B. Vegetables and water. See Daniel 1:12. Some translations, including the King James Version, specify "pulse and water" (pulses are legumes) while others more generally say "vegetables and water."

14. D. All of the above. See Genesis 18:5–8.

15. John the Baptist was said to eat these.

    A. Goat's milk and figs
    B. Grains and water
    C. Locusts and wild honey
    D. The Bible does not mention John the Baptist eating.

16. In Numbers 11, while wandering the desert after their exodus from Egypt, the Israelites complained that they missed this food from Egypt.

    A. Fish
    B. Cucumbers
    C. Melons
    D. Leeks
    E. All of the above
    F. None of the above

17. What did Jonathan eat that broke the fast that Saul had called for his army when they were fighting the Philistines?

    A. Bread dipped in vinegar
    B. Olives
    C. Honey
    D. Wheat

Answers on page 98.

Answers from previous page:

15. C. Locusts and wild honey. See Matthew 3:4 and Mark 1:6. Some scholars believe that "locusts" refer to the locust tree and its fruit, not the insect.

16. E. All of the above. See Numbers 11:5–6: "We remember the fish, which we did eat in Egypt freely; the cucumbers, and the melons, and the leeks, and the onions, and the garlick: But now our soul is dried away: there is nothing at all, beside this manna, before our eyes."

17. C. Honey. See 1 Samuel 14:24–45.

GIFTS, PAYMENTS, AND OTHER OFFERINGS

18. Isaac gave golden bracelets to Rebekah to indicate that he wanted to marry her.

    A. True

    B. False

19. In Numbers 6, the Lord decreed that people who took a vow as a Nazirite were prohibited from eating anything that came from this.

    A. The grapevine

    B. The olive tree

    C. The sea

    D. The wheat field

20. In Exodus, manna is described as tasting like this.

    A. Spices

    B. Wafers made with honey

    C. Bitter herbs

    D. Tasteless

Answers on page 100.

Answers from previous page:

18. B. False. Abraham sent a servant to find a bride for his son Isaac, and it was that servant who gave jewelry to Rebekah. See Genesis 24.

19. A. The grapevine. Numbers 6:3–4 says, "He shall separate himself from wine and strong drink, and shall drink no vinegar of wine, or vinegar of strong drink, neither shall he drink any liquor of grapes, nor eat moist grapes, or dried. All the days of his separation shall he eat nothing that is made of the vine tree, from the kernels even to the husk."

20. B. Wafers made with honey. See Exodus 16:31. In Numbers 11:8, however, it's described as tasting like "fresh oil."

GIFTS, PAYMENTS, AND OTHER OFFERINGS

21. When Joseph was in prison in Egypt, he interpreted the dreams of a butler and a baker. What did the butler dream of?

   A. Sheaves of wheat

   B. Stars, the sun, and the moon

   C. A ripe vine laden with grapes

   D. Baskets of bread

22. 1 Samuel 25 tells of a wealthy man named Nabal who provided a feast to David and his men after they had protected his shepherds and sheep.

   A. True

   B. False

23. How much money did Joseph's brothers gain when they sold him to a merchant caravan?

   A. None

   B. Seven pieces of silver

   C. 20 pieces of silver

   D. 40 pieces of silver

Answers on page 102.

Answers from previous page:

21. C. A ripe vine laden with grapes. The butler used the grapes to fill Pharaoh's cup. Genesis 40 tells the story.

22. B. False. Nabal refused to help David or his men out, which angered David. Nabal's wife, Abigail, when informed that David and his men were marching towards Nabal's lands, set out to prepare a feast for them and beg David's forgiveness.

23. C. 20 pieces of silver. See Genesis 37:28.

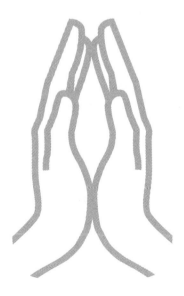

MAMMALS, REPTILES, AND BIRDS

1. From his deathbed, what animal did Jacob compare to his son Judah?

A. Raven
B. Lion
C. Lamb
D. Serpent

2. In Acts, after a shipwreck, this animal bit Paul, yet he suffered no harm.

A. A scorpion
B. A snake
C. A shark
D. A lion

Answers on page 104.

Answers from previous page:

1. B. Lion. See Genesis 49:9.

2. B. A snake. See Acts 28:3–6.

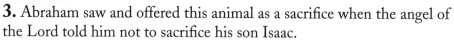

3. Abraham saw and offered this animal as a sacrifice when the angel of the Lord told him not to sacrifice his son Isaac.

    A. A kid goat

    B. A lamb

    C. A ram

    D. An ewe

4. While in Egypt, Abram acquired the following animals.

    A. Sheep

    B. Cattle

    C. Camels

    D. Donkeys

    E. All of the above

5. Jesus instructed Simon Peter to pay the temple tax by catching one of these and taking a coin from its mouth.

    A. A dove

    B. A fish

    C. A ram

    D. A pig

Answers on page 106.

Answers from previous page:

3. C. A ram. See Genesis 22:13.

4. E. All of the above. See Genesis 12:16.

5. B. A fish. See Matthew 17:27.

6. In 1 Kings 21, who did the Lord say shall be eaten by dogs?

A. Isaac
B. Bilhah
C. Jezebel
D. Samson

7. The Philistines returned the ark of the covenant to Israel by placing it in a cart and letting two unguided cows pull it. Where did the cows go?

A. Jerusalem
B. Into the sea
C. Into the wilderness
D. Bethshemesh

8. In 1 Kings 17, Elijah was brought food by this type of bird.

A. Pigeons
B. Ravens
C. Doves
D. Sparrows

Answers on page 108.

Answers from previous page:

6. C. Jezebel. In 1 Kings 21, the Lord, speaking through the prophet Elijah, said, "The dogs shall eat Jezebel by the wall of Jezreel." See 1 Kings 21:23.

7. D. Bethshemesh. See 1 Samuel 6:12.

8. B. Ravens. See 1 Kings 17:1–6.

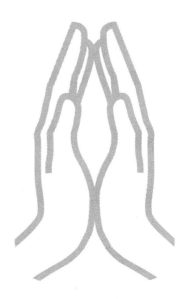

9. Which book contains the story of Balaam's donkey refusing to carry him further because the angel of the Lord was standing in their way?

   A. Numbers

   B. Deuteronomy

   C. Joshua

   D. Judges

10. In the Parable of the Prodigal Son, the older brother said bitterly that his father had never given him this.

   A. A kid goat so he could feast with his friends

   B. A sheep so he could host a celebration

   C. A fatted calf at his wedding celebration

   D. Pigeons so he could sacrifice to the Lord

11. In the story of Joseph, when Pharaoh dreamt of seven fat kine (cattle), what happened to them in the dream to indicate that famine would follow a time of plenty?

   A. The grain they were eating disappeared, leaving them to starve.

   B. They were eaten by seven lions.

   C. They were eaten by seven skinny, starving cows.

   D. They were chased away by seven skinny, starving cows.

Answers on page 110.

Answers from previous page:

9. A. Numbers. See Numbers 22.

10. A. A kid goat so he could feast with his friends. See Luke 15:29.

11. C. They were eaten by seven skinny, starving cows. See Genesis 41:1–4.

12. In Isaiah's prophecy about the root of Jesse, it is said that the wolf will dwell with the lamb, and the cow will eat safely near this animal.

    A. The leopard
    B. The bear
    C. The lion
    D. A kid goat

13. What did Daniel escape from unharmed?

    A. A pit of snakes
    B. A den of hyenas
    C. A vat of sharks
    D. A den of lions

14. Moses was tending his father-in-law Jethro's cattle when he saw the burning bush.

    A. True
    B. False

Answers on page 112.

Answers from previous page:

12. B. The bear. See Isaiah 11:6–7: "The wolf also shall dwell with the lamb, and the leopard shall lie down with the kid; and the calf and the young lion and the fatling together; and a little child shall lead them. And the cow and the bear shall feed; their young ones shall lie down together: and the lion shall eat straw like the ox."

13. D. A den of lions. See Daniel 6:22.

14. B. False. He was tending his father-in-law Jethro's sheep. See Exodus 3:1–3.

15. When Rebekah wanted to fool Isaac into believing Jacob was Esau, a "hairy man," she covered Jacob's smooth hands and neck in this material.

A. Goat skins

B. Cattle skin

C. Snakeskin

D. Lion fur

16. In one post-Resurrection appearance, Jesus came to his disciples after they'd had a night of unsuccessful fishing and told them to throw their net to the right side. How many fish did they gather in their nets when they did as he said?

A. 12

B. 40

C. 153

D. 1,000

17. Who was the king that ordered Daniel thrown into the lions' den?

A. Darius

B. Joshua

C. David

D. Hoshea

Answers on page 114.

Answers from previous page:

15. A. Goat skins. See Genesis 27:15–16: "And Rebekah took goodly raiment of her eldest son Esau, which were with her in the house, and put them upon Jacob her younger son: And she put the skins of the kids of the goats upon his hands, and upon the smooth of his neck."

16. C. 153. See John 21:1–14.

17. A. Darius. See Daniel 6.

TRAVELS BY LAND AND WATER

1. On his first journey through Greece, Paul landed in Neapolis and next went here.

A. Athens
B. Corinth
C. Philippi
D. Ephesus

2. Jacob did not send this son to Egypt for corn during the famine.

A. Asher
B. Benjamin
C. Gad
D. Zebulun

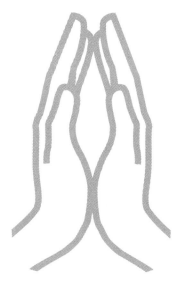

Answers on page 116.

Answers from previous page:

1. C. Philippi. See Acts 16:11–12.

2. B. Benjamin. See Genesis 42:1–4.

3. Paul's first journey to Greece is described in this book.

A. Matthew

B. Mark

C. Luke

D. Acts

4. Jonah took passage on a ship—ultimately ending up in a fish's belly for three days—to avoid God's command to go preach in this wicked city.

A. Rome

B. Jerusalem

C. Nineveh

D. Tarshish

5. In Genesis 31, God advises Jacob to flee Laban, his father-in-law. Where does he go?

A. To the land of his fathers

B. Into the wilderness

C. To the foot of Mount Zion

D. To a hiding place in Mount Carmel

Answers on page 118.

Answers from previous page:

3. D. Acts. Acts 16:9 specifically explains what incites Paul: "And a vision appeared to Paul in the night; There stood a man of Macedonia, and prayed him, saying, Come over into Macedonia, and help us."

4. C. Nineveh. The command that set off Jonah's adventure is in Jonah 1:2: "Arise, go to Nineveh, that great city, and cry against it; for their wickedness is come up before me."

5. A. To the land of his fathers. See Genesis 31:3.

6. This was one of the lands Abram passed through on his journey from Haran to Egypt.

   A. Parthia

   B. Canaan

   C. Ethiopia

   D. He travelled by sea, not land

7. After crossing the Red Sea, Moses led his people into the wilderness. What was the name of this wilderness?

   A. Moab

   B. Elim

   C. Shur

   D. Rameses

8. Which prophet fled from Beersheba to Horeb?

   A. Ezekiel

   B. Isaiah

   C. Elijah

   D. Moses

Answers on page 120.

Answers from previous page:

6. B. Canaan. See Genesis 12:5

7. C. Shur. See Exodus 15:22.

8. C. Elijah. He was fleeing the wrath of Jezebel and Ahab. See 1 Kings 19:2–3, 8.

9. At the end of his first journey through Greece, Paul spent a year and six months here.

A. Athens

B. Corinth

C. Philippi

D. Ephesus

10. Philip had just finished baptizing an Ethiopian when God abruptly carried him away to this place.

A. Jerusalem

B. A mountaintop

C. Azotus

D. The mount of Olives

11. Ezra led a group of exiles on a five-month journey from this place back to Jerusalem.

A. Nineveh

B. Egypt

C. Babylon

D. An unknown desert

Answers on page 122.

Answers from previous page:

9. B. Corinth. See Acts 18:11.

10. C. Azotus. See Acts 8:39–40.

11. C. Babylon. See Ezra 7:6–9.

12. In Acts 18, Paul sailed from Corinth to Ephesus. What modern country would Ephesus be located in?

    A. Greece
    B. Italy
    C. Slovenia
    D. Turkey

13. The book of Matthew mentions wise men that came to worship Jesus. Which direction did these travelers come from?

    A. East
    B. West
    C. North
    D. South

14. When Paul was sent to Rome for judgment, how did he travel?

    A. By ship
    B. By wagon
    C. On horseback
    D. On foot

Answers on page 124.

Answers from previous page:

12. D. Turkey. The ruins of the city are located on Turkey's western coast. See Acts 18:1, 18–19.

13. A. East. See Matthew 2:1.

14. A. By ship. See Acts 27:1.

BATTLES, KILLINGS, AND DEATH

1. When the Philistines captured the ark of the covenant, their army was camped here.

    A. Jericho
    B. Shiloh
    C. Ashdod
    D. Aphek

2. King Josiah fought King Necho of Egypt in this valley.

    A. Megiddo
    B. Jordan
    C. Eshcol
    D. Achor

Answers on page 126.

Answers from previous page:

1. D. Aphek. See 1 Samuel 4:1, 11.

2. A. Megiddo. See 2 Chronicles 35:22.

3. When Cain killed Abel, where were the two brothers?

    A. An olive grove

    B. The garden of Eden

    C. A field

    D. A temple

4. After killing Abel, where did Cain go?

    A. The land of Gog

    B. The land of Nod

5. Benhadad, the king of Syria, attacked this part of Israel during Ahab's reign.

    A. Bethel

    B. Samaria

    C. Hebron

    D. Tekoa

Answers on page 128.

Answers from previous page:

3. C. A field. See Genesis 4:8.

4. B. The land of Nod. Genesis 4:16 says, "And Cain went out from the presence of the Lord, and dwelt in the land of Nod, on the east of Eden."

5. B. Samaria. See 1 Kings 20:1.

6. Saul was jealous about a song that celebrated David's victory in battle. Fill in the blanks in the lyrics: "Saul hath slain his _____, and David his _____."

   A. Tens / Hundreds
   B. Hundreds / Thousands
   C. Thousands / Ten thousands
   D. Enemies / King's enemies

7. When Joseph's other brothers wanted to kill him, which brother argued for his life?

   A. Reuben
   B. Levi
   C. Simeon
   D. Judah

8. Saul, the king anointed by Samuel, fought his final battle here.

   A. Mount Carmel
   B. Mount Zion
   C. Mount Gilboa
   D. Mount Nebo

Answers on page 130.

Answers from previous page:

6. C. Thousands / Ten thousands. See 1 Samuel 18:7.

7. A. Reuben. See Genesis 37:21–22. Reuben says they should throw Joseph in a cistern rather than kill him. He intends to rescue him and restore him to their father Jacob later. When a caravan passes, however, Judah suggests selling Joseph to the merchants instead.

8. C. Mount Gilboa. See 1 Samuel 3:14.

9. What did Jael use to kill Sisera?

A. Tent nail
B. Poison
C. Mighty sword
D. Statue of false deity

10. Which relative intended to kill Joash as a child?

A. Uncle
B. Grandmother
C. Aunt
D. Father

11. Who killed Eglon, the king of Moab?

A. Enoch
B. Shem
C. Ehud
D. Tobias

Answers on page 132.

Answers from previous page:

9. A. Tent nail. Jael killed Sisera by driving a tent nail into his temples. See Judges 4:21–22.

10. B. Grandmother. Joash's grandmother, Athaliah, ordered the killing of Joash along with the rest of the royal family. But her plans were spoiled when Joash's aunt "stole him from among the king's sons which were slain." See 2 Kings 11:2.

11. C. Ehud. See Judges 3:15–25.

12. According to 1 Chronicles, how did King Saul die?

    A. He committed suicide.

    B. He died of old age.

    C. He was killed by the Philistines during battle.

    D. He was killed by his son Jonathan.

13. Michmash was one of the war camps used during a battle between these two groups.

    A. The Egyptians and the Edomites

    B. The Hebrews and the Philistines

14. What prophet said, "Jeroboam shall die by the sword, and Israel shall surely be led away captive out of their own land"?

    A. Amos

    B. Jonah

    C. Nathan

    D. Obadiah

Answers on page 134.

Answers from previous page:

12. A. He committed suicide. After being wounded by the Philistines' archers, King Saul asked his armorbearer to kill him. When the armorbearer refused, Saul fell upon his sword. See 1 Chronicles 10:3–4.

13. B. The Hebrews and the Philistines. Michmash is mentioned several times in this context in 1 Samuel. 1 Samuel 13:5 notes that the Philistines "came up, and pitched in Michmash."

14. A. Amos. See Amos 7:11.

15. What son of King David died when he was hung on a tree by his hair?

    A. Absalom

    B. Daniel

    C. Shimea

    D. Amnon

16. Which book tells the story of how Joshua led the Israelites in battle against the Amalekites while Moses held the staff of God, so that whenever Moses held up his arms, the Israelites were victorious?

    A. Exodus

    B. Numbers

    C. Deuteronomy

    D. Joshua

17. Genesis mentions a battle that took place in the vale of Siddim between multiple kings. An invading Egyptian army caused the battle.

    A. True

    B. False

Answers on page 136.

Answers from previous page:

15. A. Absalom. Absalom was riding a mule when his hair became tangled in an oak tree. His mule left, so Absalom hung from the tree by his hair. See 2 Samuel 18:9–10.

16. A. Exodus. See Exodus 17:8–13.

17. B. False. Genesis 14 explains that the kings were rebelling against Chedorlaomer, a king of Elam.

18. Og, the king of Bashan, attacked the Israelites here during the Exodus.

   A. Edrei
   B. Samaria
   C. Megiddo
   D. Bashan city

19. Which book contains the story of the Lord turning against Saul for failing to follow the Lord's instructions in the battle against the Amalekites?

   A. Judges
   B. 1 Samuel
   C. 2 Samuel
   D. 1 Kings

20. The first battle mentioned in the Bible took place in Genesis 14. It is associated with this place name.

   A. A. The vale of Siddim
   B. B. The valley of Eshcol

Answers on page 138.

Answers from previous page:

18. A. Edrei. See Numbers 21:33.

19. B. 1 Samuel. See 1 Samuel 15.

20. A. The vale of Siddim. See Genesis 14:3, 8, 10.

21. Thanks to an ambush suggested by God, Joshua was able to destroy this city.

A. Ai
B. Jerusalem
C. Jericho
D. Jebus

22. Which woman threatened to kill Elijah after he put the prophets of Baal to death?

A. Jezebel
B. Mary
C. Sarah
D. Delilah

23. After killing an Egyptian, Moses fled from the wrath of Pharaoh to this land.

A. Canaan
B. Syria
C. Midian
D. Aram

Answers on page 140.

Answers from previous page:

21 A. Ai. In Joshua 8 we learn that 30,000 of Joshua's men hid behind a hill while the rest of the Israelites drew out the people of Ai. Once the city was deserted, Joshua's men set it on fire.

22. A. Jezebel. After Ahab delivered the news that Elijah had killed the prophets of Baal, Jezebel sent a messenger to Elijah threatening him with death. See 1 Kings 19:1–2.

23. C. Midian. Midian was a region located in the northwestern Arabian Desert. See Exodus 2:15.

24. Who consented to the execution of the first Christian martyr?

   A. Saul
   B. Peter
   C. John the Baptist
   D. Thomas

25. While fighting a wearying battle with the Philistines, David longed for water from this specific well.

   A. The well of Bethlehem
   B. The well of the Philistines

26. Where did David slay Goliath?

   A. On a hill above the valley of Succoth
   B. In Jehoshaphat valley
   C. In the valley of Elah
   D. The location is unknown.

Answers on page 142.

Answers from previous page:

24. A. Saul. Saul consented to and witnessed Stephen's death. Saul would later become the apostle Paul and one of the greatest missionaries. See Acts 8:1.

25. A. The well of Bethlehem. See 2 Samuel 23:15.

26. C. In the valley of Elah. See 1 Samuel 21:9. The story of the battle itself is related in 1 Samuel 17.

SON OF GOD

1. Jesus crossed this brook into a garden on the night that he was betrayed by Judas.

    A. Kishron
    B. Pishon
    C. Cedron
    D. None of the above

2. Who did Herod send to Bethlehem to search for the young Christ child?

    A. High priests
    B. Scribes
    C. Wise men
    D. John the Baptist

Answers on page 144.

Answers from previous page:

1. C. Cedron. See John 18:1.

2. C. Wise men. According to the Gospel of Matthew, the wise men came looking for the child born "King of the Jews." When Herod heard this, he asked the wise men when the star appeared. Herod asked them to return word once they found the child so that he could worship him also. But the wise men were warned in a dream not to return to Herod, so they went home another way. See Matthew 2:1–12.

3. Jesus went to Rome to convert Gentiles.

    A. True

    B. False

4. Jesus returned to Egypt as an adult to preach to the Egyptians.

    A. True

    B. False

5. Jesus met his disciples James and John while they were mending nets in a ship on this sea.

    A. The Sea of Galilee

    B. The Dead Sea

    C. The Bible does not specify a sea.

    D. None of the above

Answers on page 146.

Answers from previous page:

3. B. False. Jesus never went to Rome.

4. B. False. Jesus did not go to Egypt as an adult.

5. A. The Sea of Galilee. See Matthew 4:21.

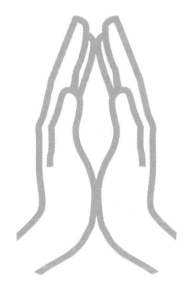

6. Which disciple tried to walk on water, as Jesus did?

    A. James (son of Zebedee)
    B. Bartholomew
    C. (Simon) Peter
    D. Andrew

7. How many jars of water did Jesus change to wine at the wedding of Cana?

    A. One
    B. Three
    C. Six
    D. 12

8. What was Jesus called in Revelation 5:5?

    A. Capstone
    B. Horn of salvation
    C. Lion of the tribe of Judah
    D. Man of sorrows

Answers on page 148.

Answers from previous page:

6. C. (Simon) Peter. See Matthew 14:25–31.

7. C. Six. See John 2:6.

8. C. Lion of the tribe of Judah. There are hundreds of names for Jesus in the Bible. In Revelation 5:5, Jesus was called "the Lion of the tribe of Judah, the Root of David."

9. Jesus chided the disciples for falling asleep in this garden.

A. Galilee

B. Golgotha

C. Gethsemane

D. Glory

10. This empire ruled Jerusalem during Jesus' time.

A. Egypt

B. Macedonia

C. Rome

D. Babylon

11. Where did Jesus go to face the devil's temptation?

A. The wilderness

B. Back to Nazareth

C. Babylon

D. The Bible does not say.

Answers on page 150.

Answers from previous page:

9. C. Gethsemane. See Matthew 26:40.

10. C. Rome.

11. A. The wilderness. See Matthew 4:1, Mark 1:12, and Luke 4:1.

12. In Mark 8:29, Peter tells Jesus, "Thou art the Christ" near this location.

    A. The mount of Olives

    B. Caesarea Philippi

    C. Bethlehem

    D. Gethsemane

13. Where did Jesus ask the Samaritan woman for a drink of water?

    A. At the well of Beersheba

    B. At the well of Jacob

14. Which disciple protested when Jesus was going to wash his feet?

    A. Thomas

    B. Andrew

    C. (Simon) Peter

    D. Matthew

Answers on page 152.

Answers from previous page:

12. B. Caesarea Philippi. See Mark 8:27.

13. B. At the well of Jacob. See John 4:6.

14. C. (Simon) Peter. See John 13:5–8.

15. What follower of Jesus requested his body for burial?

  A. Joseph (of Arimathaea)
  B. Simon
  C. Mary Magdalene
  D. James (son of Alphaeus)

16. Who fell to Jesus' knees and said, "Depart from me; for I am a sinful man, O Lord"?

  A. Andrew
  B. Simon Peter
  C. Moses
  D. Didymus

17. The Sermon on the Mount refers to a sermon Jesus gave on Mount Zion.

  A. True
  B. False

Answers on page 154.

Answers from previous page:

15. A. Joseph (of Arimathaea). See Matthew 27:57–58, Mark 15:43–44, Luke 23:50–52, and John 19:38.

16. B. Simon Peter. Simon Peter said this after seeing Jesus perform a miracle with a draught of fish. See Luke 5:3–9.

17. B. False. The exact location of Jesus' Sermon on the Mount is not known.

18. Jesus was crucified at a place called Golgotha. What does this name mean?

    A. Place of olives
    B. Place of bones
    C. Place of a goat
    D. Place of a skull

19. Simon of Cyrene was forced by the Roman soldiers to carry Jesus' cross up to Golgotha.

    A. True
    B. False

20. Jesus found Matthew sitting here and asked him to become his disciple.

    A. A city gate of Jerusalem
    B. A centurion's storehouse
    C. A tax collector's station
    D. Near a fishing boat

Answers on page 156.

Answers from previous page:

18. D. Place of a skull. See Matthew 27:33, Mark 15:22, and John 19:17.

19. A. True. See Matthew 27:31–32.

20. C. A tax collector's station. See Matthew 9:9.

21. Where was Jesus born?

    A. Jerusalem

    B. Rome

    C. Nazareth

    D. Bethlehem

22. Jesus told the Parable of the Rich Fool in response to this event.

    A. A wealthy man expressed the desire to follow him.

    B. One of his disciples expressed a desire for wealth.

    C. A man in the crowd wanted Jesus to tell the man's brother to share a family inheritance.

    D. The Bible doesn't say what prompted the parable.

23. After feeding the multitude in Mark 8:1–9, Jesus took a ship to Dalmanutha. Joshua, King Saul, and Elijah also visited this town.

    A. True

    B. False

Answers on page 158.

Answers from previous page:

21. D. Bethlehem. Jesus' birthplace is referenced in multiple places in the Bible. For example, Matthew 2:1 says, "Now when Jesus was born in Bethlehem of Judaea in the days of Herod the king, behold, there came wise men from the east to Jerusalem."

22. C. A man in the crowd wanted Jesus to tell the man's brother to share a family inheritance. Jesus responded by telling the crowd a parable that illustrated the dangers of concentrating on earthly wealth instead of their relationship with God.

23. B. False. Mark 8:10 is the only verse in the Bible that mentions Dalmanutha.

PENALTIES AND PUNISHMENTS

1. In Cyprus, when Paul was teaching an official and a sorcerer and a false prophet interfered, Paul said this would be his punishment.

   A. He would be blinded.

   B. He would become leprous.

   C. He would become mute.

   D. He would die.

2. In Daniel, what was the penalty for not worshipping the golden statue that Nebuchadnezzar had raised whenever "ye hear the sound of the cornet, flute, harp, sackbut, psaltery, dulcimer, and all kinds of musick"?

   A. To be thrown in a lion's den

   B. To be thrown in a fiery furnace

   C. To be imprisoned without bread and water

   D. To be cut in pieces and your house made a dunghill

Answers on page 160.

Answers from previous page:

1. A. He would be blinded. See Acts 13:6–12.

2. B. To be thrown in a fiery furnace. See Daniel 3:4-6. Shadrach, Meshach, and Abednego paid that penalty but went unharmed, astonishing Nebuchadnezzar.

3. Who prophesied that the Lord would punish the kings of the earth by gathering them together as prisoners in a pit?

   A. Isaiah
   B. Jeremiah
   C. Gideon
   D. Barnabas

4. What lie was told about Naboth in 1 Kings 21?

   A. He had blasphemed against God.
   B. He had worshipped an idol.
   C. He had committed incest with his daughter.
   D. He had cured a leper.

5. In Colossians, Paul stated that he was writing the letter from prison.

   A. True
   B. False

Answers on page 162.

Answers from previous page:

3. A. Isaiah. See Isaiah 24:21–22.

4. A. He had blasphemed against God. See 1 Kings 21:10.

5. A. True. See Colossians 4:10, which references a fellow prisoner, and his closing note in 4:18.

6. A great flood occurred while Paul and Silas were imprisoned in Philippi.

    A. True
    B. False

7. What notable prisoner was released when Jesus was sentenced to death?

    A. Cleopas
    B. Judas
    C. Pilate
    D. Barabbas

8. The prophet Ezekiel experienced his visions while in captivity here.

    A. The land of the Egyptians
    B. The land of the Chaldeans
    C. The land of the Moabites
    D. The land of the Samaritans

Answers on page 164.

Answers from previous page:

6. B. False. While Paul and Silas were imprisoned in Philippi, a great earthquake shook the foundation of the prison. Even though the doors were opened, Paul and Silas refused to flee, which prompted the jail keeper to ask them what he needed to do to be saved. See Acts 16:25–30.

7. D. Barabbas. See Matthew 27:16–26, Mark 15:15, Luke 23:18–24, and John 19:39–40.

8. B. The land of the Chaldeans. See Ezekiel 1:3.

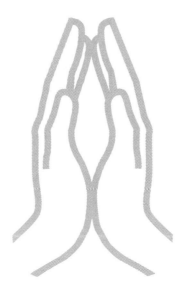

9. Where did the 70-year captivity mentioned in Jeremiah 29 take place?

A. Egypt

B. Nineveh

C. Babylon

D. Damascus

10. When Joseph accuses Benjamin of theft, which brother offers to fulfill Benjamin's punishment in his stead?

A. Reuben

B. Levi

C. Simeon

D. Judah

11. Nebuchadnezzar took his captives from Jerusalem to this place.

A. Damascus

B. Babylon

C. Rome

D. Egypt

Answers on page 166.

Answers from previous page:

9. C. Babylon. See Jeremiah 29:1–10.

10. D. Judah. See Genesis 44:14–33.

11. B. Babylon. See Jeremiah 29:1.

REMEDIES AND MIRACLES

1. What was the name of Jairus' daughter, who was raised from the dead?

   A. Joanna
   B. Tabitha
   C. Susanna
   D. She wasn't named.

2. God provided this to Jonah while he waited to see what would happen to Ninevah.

   A. Food to sustain him
   B. A spring of water
   C. A vine to shade him
   D. A ram to make sacrifice

Answers on page 168.

Answers from previous page:

1. D. She wasn't named. Jairus, the synagogue leader, didn't refer to her by name. When raising her, Jesus called her a "damsel" in the Gospel of Mark and a "maid" in Matthew and Luke. See Matthew 9:18, 23–26; Mark 5:22–23, 35–42; and Luke 8:41–42, 49–55.

2. C. A vine to shade him. See Jonah 4:6.

3. Mark 8:22–26 describes Jesus healing a blind man with this substance.

    A. Tears

    B. Spit

    C. Mud

    D. Nothing—he healed the blind man from afar

4. Whose mother-in-law did Jesus heal?

    A. (Simon) Peter

    B. Nicodemus

    C. A centurion

    D. Bartholomew

5. When Elisha restored the son of the Shunammite woman to life, what was the first thing the boy did?

    A. Gave thanks to the Lord

    B. Sneezed

    C. Rose from his sickbed

    D. Ate some bread dipped in oil

Answers on page 170.

Answers from previous page:

3. B. Spit. See Mark 8:23: "And he took the blind man by the hand, and led him out of the town; and when he had spit on his eyes, and put his hands upon him, he asked him if he saw ought."

4. A. (Simon) Peter. See Matthew 8:14–15, Mark 1:29–31, and Luke 4:38–39.

5. B. Sneezed. See 2 Kings 4:35: " Then he [Elisha] returned, and walked in the house to and fro; and went up, and stretched himself upon him: and the child sneezed seven times, and the child opened his eyes."

6. The book of Acts describes how Paul prayed to restore the disciple Dorcas, also known as Tabitha, to life.

    A. True
    B. False

7. Elijah gave instructions for the healing of Naaman, the commander of the army of Syria, from leprosy.

    A. True
    B. False

8. When Elijah was taken up to heaven, he left this behind for Elisha.

    A. A staff
    B. A cloak
    C. His sandals
    D. Nothing

Answers on page 172.

Answers from previous page:

6. B. False. It was Peter, not Paul. See Acts 9:36–42.

7. B. False. It was Elisha; see 2 Kings 5.

8. B. A cloak. See 2 Kings 2:13: "He took up also the mantle of Elijah that fell from him, and went back, and stood by the bank of Jordan."

9. A Canaanite woman pleaded with Jesus to heal her daughter, even though they weren't Israelites. What was the daughter's affliction?

A. Lameness

B. Internal bleeding

C. Possession by an unclean spirit

D. Blindness

10. When Jesus restored the son of the widow of Nain to life, he did so in response to this.

A. She found him and pleaded with him.

B. Her friends came on her behalf.

C. He saw the funeral procession and felt compassion for her.

D. One of the disciples asked if Jesus could help her.

11. Lazarus had been buried for this period of time when Jesus came to Bethany to raise him from the dead.

A. One day

B. Three days

C. Four days

D. Seven days

Answers on page 174.

Answers from previous page:

9. C. Possession by an unclean spirit. See Mark 7:25 or Matthew 15:22.

10. C. He saw the funeral procession and felt compassion for her. See Luke 7:11–17.

11. C. Four days. See John 11:17.

12. After Jesus healed Simon Peter's mother-in-law, the first thing she did was this.

    A. She anointed Jesus' feet with oil.
    B. She served Jesus and his disciples.
    C. She offered a sacrifice at the temple.
    D. The Bible doesn't say.

13. Which woman did Peter raise from the dead at Lydda?

    A. Phebe
    B. Miriam
    C. Euodia
    D. Tabitha

14. Where did Jesus heal the Roman centurion's servant?

    A. Shiloh
    B. Bethel
    C. Capernaum
    D. Chorazin

Answers on page 176.

Answers from previous page:

12. B. She served Jesus and his disciples. See Matthew 8:14–15, Mark 1:29–31, and Luke 4:38–39.

13. D. Tabitha. Peter brought Tabitha, who was also known as Dorcas, back to life. See Acts 9:36–41.

14. C. Capernaum. See Matthew 8:5–13 and Luke 7:1–10.

15. Jesus brought a dead man back to life near the gates of a city called Nain.

   A. True
   B. False

16. Jesus gave a blind man sight by anointing his eyes with clay and then telling him to wash his eyes here.

   A. The well of Jacob
   B. The pool of Siloam
   C. The well of Nazareth
   D. In a nearby river

17. Which book tells the story of Isaiah healing Hezekiah the king with a poultice of figs?

   A. 1 Kings
   B. 2 Kings
   C. 1 Chronicles
   D. None of the above

Answers on page 178.

Answers from previous page:

15. A. True. See Luke 7:11–15.

16. B. The pool of Siloam. See John 9:1–11.

17. B. See 2 Kings 20:1–7. The story is also told in Isaiah 38.

18. Who raised Eutychus from the dead?

A. Jesus
B. Elijah
C. Paul
D. Peter

19. Jesus performed his first miracle in this town.

A. Capernaum
B. Canaan
C. Calneh
D. Cana

20. The book of Acts describes how handkerchiefs or items of clothing that touched Paul would heal the sick.

A. True
B. False

Answers on page 180.

Answers from previous page:

18. C. Paul. After Eutychus fell from a window during Paul's sermon and died, Paul brought him back to life. See Acts 20:9–10.

19. D. Cana. While attending a wedding in Cana, Jesus changed six pots of water into wine. See John 2:1–11.

20. A. True. See Acts 19:11–12.

SONGS AND CELEBRATIONS

1. In 1 Chronicles 15:19, Heman, Asaph, and Ethan were appointed to sound with which musical instruments?

   A. Trumpets of gold

   B. Harps

   C. Cymbals of brass

   D. Viols (lyres)

2. Jericho's defensive wall fell down after Joshua sent seven priests to sing before its gate.

   A. True

   B. False

Answers on page 182.

Answers from previous page:

1. C. Cymbals of brass. The Levites appointed Heman (son of Joel), Asaph (son of Berechiah), and Ethan (son of Kushaiah) to be the singers with instruments of music "to sound with cymbals of brass." See 1 Chronicles 15:16–17, 19.

2. B. False. In Joshua 6, we learn that six days of trumpet-blowing perambulations took place before the wall came down. When the priests blew their trumpets on the seventh day, the people joined in with their own shouting—and Jericho's wall collapsed.

3. 1 Kings 4, speaking of Solomon's wisdom, says that he created 3,000 proverbs and more than 1,000 songs.

    A. True
    B. False

4. Paul instructed his readers to include music in their worship.

    A. True
    B. False

5. "For the Lord's portion is his people; Jacob is the lot of his inheritance. He found him in a desert land, and in the waste howling wilderness; he led him about, he instructed him, he kept him as the apple of his eye." Who shared the song containing this verse with Israel, and on what occasion?

    A. Moses, after the Israelites crossed the Red Sea
    B. Moses, shortly before his death
    C. David, on his coronation
    D. Solomon, on his coronation

Answers on page 184.

Answers from previous page:

3. A. True. See 1 Kings 4:32–34 for a list of Solomon's accomplishments, which included proverbs, songs, and extensive knowledge of plant and animal life.

4. A. True. See Colossians 3:16: " Let the word of Christ dwell in you richly in all wisdom; teaching and admonishing one another in psalms and hymns and spiritual songs, singing with grace in your hearts to the Lord." There's a similar exhortation in Ephesians 5:18–19.

5. B. Moses, shortly before his death. In Deuteronomy 31, the Lord instructed Moses to write the song and teach it to the children of Israel. For the verses quoted, see Deuteronomy 32:9-10.

6. In Revelation 5:13, who is described as singing, "Blessing, and honor, and glory, and power, be unto him that sitteth upon the throne, and unto the Lamb"?

   A. The 24 elders gathered around the throne

   B. 10,000 angels

   C. Every creature which is in heaven, and on the earth, and under the earth, and such as are in the sea

   D. The author of the book

7. When Miriam led the women in song and dance after the Israelites crossed the Red Sea, she used this instrument.

   A. A timbrel, or tambourine

   B. A flute

   C. A drum

   D. A lyre, or harp

8. Which woman sang a celebration song with Barak after the downfall of Sisera?

   A. Tamar

   B. Deborah

   C. Naomi

   D. Dinah

Answers on page 186.

Answers from previous page:

6. C. Every creature which is in heaven, and on the earth, and under the earth, and such as are in the sea. Revelation 5 describes a group of 24 elders and four creatures who sing a song; they are joined by a multitude of angels, and finally, in the verse in the question, by every creature in heaven and on earth.

7. A. A timbrel, or tambourine. See Exodus 15:20.

8. B. Deborah. After the downfall of Sisera, Deborah and Barak sang and praised God for avenging Israel. See Judges 5:1–3.

9. Both Mark and Matthew describe Jesus and his disciples singing a hymn on this occasion.

A. On entering Jerusalem for the Passover

B. At the close of the dinner at Simon's house in Bethany

C. At the beginning of the Lord's Supper

D. At the end of the Lord's Supper, before going to the Mount of Olives

10. Mary's song concluded with these lines: "to give light to them that sit in darkness and in the shadow of death, to guide our feet into the way of peace."

A. True

B. False

11. When an evil spirit tormented Saul, this would soothe him.

A. David would play on the flute.

B. David would play on the harp (lyre).

C. His son Jonathan would play on the harp (lyre).

D. His daughter Michal would sing to him.

Answers on page 188.

Answers from previous page:

9. D. At the end of the Lord's Supper, before going to the Mount of Olives. See Matthew 26:30 and Mark 14:26.

10. B. False. The lines conclude the prophecy of Zechariah (Zacharias) when his son John the Baptist was born. See Luke 1:67–79.

11. B. David would play on the harp. See 1 Samuel 16:14–23.

12. Under David's kingship, 288 men were set aside for "song in the house of the Lord, with cymbals, psalteries, and harps."

    A. True
    B. False

13. Solomon learned that his brother, Adonijah, was claiming the throne because he heard the sound of trumpets and rejoicing from the people.

    A. True
    B. False

14. James 5:13 says that believers should "sing psalms" on these occasions.

    A. When they're gathered together
    B. When they're afflicted
    C. When they're merry
    D. When they're sick

Answers on page 190.

Answers from previous page:

12. A. True. See 1 Chronicles 25:7.

13. B. False. Adonijah set himself up to be king, but Bathsheba and Nathan persuaded David to arrange for Solomon to succeed him. After Solomon was anointed as king, there was a procession with trumpets and pipes. It was Adonijah who heard the sounds of celebration and learned that it was because of Solomon's anointing. See 1 Kings 1.

14. C. When they're merry. The full verse advises: "Is any among you afflicted? let him pray. Is any merry? let him sing psalms."

15. When Deborah and Barak sang after the victory over Sisera, the song ended with this line.

    A. "They ceased in Israel, until that I Deborah arose, that I arose a mother in Israel."

    B. "Awake, awake, Deborah: awake, awake, utter a song: arise, Barak."

    C. "The mother of Sisera looked out at a window, and cried through the lattice, Why is his chariot so long in coming?"

    D. "So let all thine enemies perish, O Lord; but let them that love him be as the sun when he goeth forth in his might."

16. The Song of Solomon ends with one of the lovers urging the other to do this.

    A. "Make haste, my beloved, and be thou like to a roe or to a young hart upon the mountain of spices."

    B. "Let us get up early to the vineyards."

    C. "Set me a seal upon thine heart."

    D. "Rise up, my love, my fair one, and come away."

17. Which prophetess said, "Sing ye to the Lord, for he hath triumphed gloriously; the horse and his rider hath he thrown into the sea" and led the women of Israel in a dance?

    A. Anna

    B. Miriam

    C. Noadiah

    D. Huldah

Answers on page 192.

Answers from previous page:

15. D. "So let all thine enemies perish, O Lord; but let them that love him be as the sun when he goeth forth in his might." See Judges 5 for the song, and Judges 5:31 for the quoted line.

16. A. "Make haste, my beloved, and be thou like to a roe or to a young hart upon the mountain of spices." See Song of Solomon 8:14. Option B is from 7:12, option C from 8:6, and option D from 2:10.

17. B. Miriam. See Exodus 15:19–21.